AF824618

What Our Readers Have Said...

Applicability

"These books are great tools that should be used as guidelines for our everyday supervisory practices. You need to take the time to do a short self-evaluation when reading them."

•

"The Pinpoint Training Series delivers information that could be used in a lot different areas."

•

"The things and problems we deal with everyday are discussed in these books."

Convenience

"I like this because I can take them with me to read at a convenient time. I feel the little time I have to spend in the office is best use on activities that directly relate to revenue opportunities. I like the short amount of time it takes to keep up with these."

•

"I prefer the self-study approach; it fits in with my schedule."

•

"I like the fact that the format allows the books to be reviewed as time permits. All work has been conducted on personal, evening/weekend time."

•

"Easy to use... if you put the time into it."

Challenge

"My thought is that the real value of these books comes into effect when doing the action plans."

•

"I like the fact that the format allows assignments to be reviewed as time permits."

Clarity

"Short and sweet. These books are easy to comprehend."

•

"Easy to use, understand, and reference if needed."

Relevance

"I have enjoyed reading these books. They are relevant to today's work environment and the ongoing change in the way we manage our workforce."

•

"I believe the contents of the Pinpoint series are excellent. It causes one to reflect on the daily dynamics in working with oneself as well as with management and peers."

Dealing with the Challenges of Leadership

Pinpoint Leadership Skill Development Training Series

TIMOTHY F. BEDNARZ

MAJORIUM
BUSINESS PRESS

Pinpoint Leadership Skill Development Training Series
"Dealing with the Challenges of Leadership"
Timothy F. Bednarz

Graphic design: Monika Pawlak

Majorium Business Press
2025 Main Street
Stevens Point, WI 54481
715.342.1018 • 800.654.4935

Copyright © 2011 Timothy F. Bednarz, Ph.D. All rights reserved. No part of this publication may be reproduced, distributed or transmitted in any form or by any means, including photocopying, recording, or other electronic or mechanical methods, without author's written permission.

ISBN 978-1-882181-68-1

Printed in the United States of America

Introduction

The Pinpoint Leadership Skill Development Training Series is designed for targeted training and education regarding increased improvement in a specific skill or competency.

Each book within this series is designed to be easy to use, understand and apply to your job. It can be used as a basis for training individuals, as a discussion guide or as a personal training tool.

Each chapter within this book discusses a specific concept. When you have completed all eight chapters you should have a 360° perspective of the topic.

Additionally, each chapter is divided into specific sections:

- The first section provides you with an overview of the topic
- The Implications section discusses why the concept is important, and why it is important to learn and apply.
- The Strategies, Tips & Techniques to Apply section teaches how to use and apply the particular concept to your work.
- The Points to Ponder section gives you something to think about or to be discussed with a group setting. These are questions not meant to be immediately answered, but to be pondered over time.
- The Training Activity section provides you with the tools to transfer what you have learned to your job. It is designed to help create an action plan to effectively apply the concept.

Each of the topics in this series is time-tested and proven in the marketplace. They have been used by thousands of employees as training tools. Many of the users have commented that what made these books valuable, was the ability to refer to them when a problem surfaced. They indicated that they remembered reading about the exact problem. They referred back to these books and found an appropriate solution.

You will find them equally valuable as a resource in your professional development library.

Table of Contents

LEARNING OBJECTIVES:

- To identify the elements and factors that create leadership challenges.
- How to overcome the problems and pitfalls associated with leadership challenges.
- How to apply effective strategies to overcome challenges in the workplace.
- To analyze cause and effect relationships of leadership challenges.
- To identify the expected results and outcomes of addressing leadership challenges and overcoming them.

1

Challenges Confronting the Leader

The role of the leader can be frustrating due to the slow speed at which organizations can evolve, react and adapt to circumstances impacting them. The primary challenge he or she faces during the ongoing process often comes from within the organization. Often, more effort is expended on stifling leadership than on encouraging it. Yet part of the challenge is to help construct an environment where leaders lead rather than merely manage.

Leaders can emerge from any level of the organization. Some may be in senior positions, with control over vast corporate resources, while others may manage only their own responsibilities. Many capable of leading and inspiring employees begin to emerge from within the ranks as the culture of empowerment slowly develops. As leaders begin to link more and compete less with other various level leaders in the organization, a synergy is created that infuses the workplace with vigor and energy. Employees feel better connected to the purpose and vision of the organization and exhibit more energy and flair in even their most routine duties. This synergy gradually overcomes many organizations' inertia and resistance toward change.

IMPLICATIONS – WHAT THIS MEANS TO YOU

Internal opposition to change is often the biggest challenge leaders face as they develop their leadership skills. They must remain committed to the principles of leadership and understand it takes time to bring about appreciable change. Facilitating change is only possible if leaders remain determined and persistent in their actions. This is the burden and commitment of leadership.

STRATEGIES, TIPS & TECHNIQUES TO APPLY

Leaders that emerge from within an organization are faced with a number of challenges, many of which may on the surface seem to go beyond the scope of their duties. However, the primary task of leaders is to create a culture in which leadership flourishes in the midst of adversity. This makes for a dramatic transformation in corporate culture and direction. The challenges facing organizations in the 21st century are inevitable and should be viewed as an impetus for progress whereby both the company and its people can succeed. These include:

Defining the Organization's Mission

Senior leadership normally defines an organization's mission. However, many organizations are compelled to rethink their mission in light of evolving competitive environments, rapidly changing technologies and the subsequent internal pressures they create.

As leaders begin to bring about change that creates a leadership-friendly and responsive environment, they have the ability to impact and ultimately redefine the organization's mission.

Creating a Flexible Environment

Leaders impact the evolution and transition of their own division or unit. As individual leaders create a more flexible environment within their respective areas of influence, incremental changes slowly affect the corporate culture. Employees are not only valued but highly respected for their contributions, treated as equals rather than underlings, and encouraged to develop to their potential.

Reshaping the Corporate Culture

As leaders bring about incremental changes within the organization, they begin to impact and reshape the entire corporate culture. Creativity, autonomy and continuous learning displace conformity, obedience and traditional training. The emergence of autonomous units under the direction of effective leaders transforms the organization from a rigid pyramid structure into a fluid circle that allows them to be more flexible, resilient and adaptable to change.

Additionally, rather than short-term profits, leaders focus the organization on long-term growth and stability. As seen in numerous corporate meltdowns, focus on short-term (and in fact often imaginary) profits can plunge companies into extreme difficulty.

Making New Connections and Alliances

As leaders grow and emerge within the organization, their initial role may be one of an influencer to promote change. This continues until their position is solidified within the organization. In this capacity, leaders are constantly making new connections to strengthen their leadership role and to develop a synergy with other leaders and employees. Not only do leaders expand their influence within the organization, they seek ways to form new alliances with external partners. Leadership is always seeking new regional and national strategic alliances to build and support the entire organization and provide additional sources of information to tap into. Emerging leaders also think globally, gaining extensive insight into how world markets, events and economies impact the organization. This enables individual leaders to put local issues and problems into perspective and understand how they impact the organization's global position.

Identifying Organizational Needs and Innovative Solutions

As leaders join together to effect internal change, they begin to identify all areas of weaknesses in their own units. Once identified, they actively work to repair and overcome them in order to avoid future problems. As world events, economies, markets and technologies impact organizations, new and unprecedented needs begin to surface, challenging individual leaders to find innovative solutions never tried before.

Being Proactive

One of the biggest challenges most emerging leaders face is gaining the ability to think proactively and develop a sense of comfort within an atmosphere of ambiguity and uncertainty. They must learn to function and compete effectively within this environment.

Most individuals are comfortable with known and established facts and rules. They function comfortably when routines are consistent, undisturbed and unchanged. While this might have been the norm in the past, the future promises even more complexity and ambiguity. Companies that once dominated their industries can rapidly see a reversal of fortunes as demonstrated by the demise of Enron and Arthur Andersen. This is also true of companies conducting all of their affairs honestly. Emerging leaders must become comfortable in this new transitional, turbulent environment and learn to adapt and succeed in the face of constant change.

In order to anticipate future events and trends, leaders analyze and interpret all available pertinent facts and data on their industry, company and unit. They also share their insights and perspectives with other leaders on all levels, in order to enable the organization as a whole to adequately prepare for future changes and opportunities.

POINTS TO PONDER – SOMETHING TO THINK ABOUT

1. As a leader, do you feel you play only a minor role that has little or no impact on your organization?
2. What leadership challenges do you see yourself facing and having to overcome as your organization evolves?

TRAINING ACTIVITY – APPLICATION & ACTION PLAN

1. Define the leadership challenges you face within your organization.
2. Identify ways you can effect or influence change.
3. Determine the impact of one incremental change you can bring about. Identify how it could positively alter your organization.
4. Identify possible alliances with other leaders outside of the organization.
5. Determine how these alliances can impact further change.

2

Common Leadership Frustrations

Some individuals are natural leaders and automatically "take point" in any and all situations. Others must make a conscious choice to do so, possibly having reluctantly accepted an unexpected leadership role. These individuals are faced with a number of choices having a direct impact on their personal and professional lives.

Active leadership takes individual courage, passion and conviction. The role requires challenging established positions and procedures. It not only places the spotlight on leaders' behaviors but also puts them under increased scrutiny by others who may not want them to succeed.

Individuals in this position cannot afford to take the path of least resistance. This is when leaders must face difficult choices with real implications for their professional and personal lives. It is not uncommon for emerging leaders to question their own motives and abilities once placed under extreme stress and pressure.

IMPLICATIONS — WHAT THIS MEANS TO YOU

A leader is motivated by an inward desire to do the best they can to maximize both their employees' efforts and overall organizational performance. While discomfort with increased scrutiny is natural, they must be able to continually persist and press forward toward their goals through adversity.

Effective leaders know they have to take a stand for necessary and essential changes if their organization is to become more competitive, develop inward strength and stability and prosper. It is the "weight" of leadership for a reason, but a necessary burden or challenge for those who see possibilities, opportunities and organizational potential.

STRATEGIES, TIPS & TECHNIQUES TO APPLY

The most common frustrations experienced by leaders are demonstrated in the contrasting roles of leaders and traditional managers.

Innovation

Managers are generally administrators of jobs and responsibilities. Leaders are organizational innovators. This means they are constantly identifying and implementing new creative concepts, principles and methods to enhance organizational effectiveness.

Managers typically copy and apply actions and methods known to work. Leaders continually develop new and original ideas. They try things that at times will not work or may even produce unexpected consequences.

Focus on People

Traditional managers tend to maintain the status quo and focus on systems and structures preserving their authority and control. This is an immediate frame of reference predicated upon short-term results and employees as workers with a job. Conversely, leaders pursue in-depth programs around developing their people's potential. They make a concerted and ongoing effort to build trust and inspire confidence.

This means leaders must deal with resistant bureaucracies and the managers therein who are threatened by change and innovation. They must be willing to deal with opposition from employees and unions used to working under strictly controlled conditions and the barriers thrown in their way to frustrate their efforts and forward movement.

Change is not an easy process, especially when dealing with individuals fearful of its possible outcomes. Leaders must learn to deal with these frustrations and develop strategies to overcome them.

Differences in Style

A wide gulf exists between a typical managerial and leadership style. Traditional managers tend to ask "how and when," leaders, "what and why." As innovators, leaders continually question the status quo and challenge its premise, especially when it interferes with their employees' ability to perform to their potential. Most are labeled troublemakers or rebels, rather than members of the team to be trusted and respected by upper management.

Leadership exacts a personal price. Leaders stand up for and do the right thing regardless of repercussions. They may not be popular, or at times even wanted within their respective organizations. Often their efforts go unappreciated for long periods of time. However, true leaders continually stand up for what they believe in, relying on their personal visions, knowing in the end the results they and their employees produce will more than negate detractors' tiresome objections.

Though working hard to meet what is expected of them, traditional managers tend to do as told without questioning the purpose of particular directives.

- Even if they do not agree with a particular direction, they rarely openly challenge it.
- They keep their eyes on the bottom line, knowing that as long as they do what they are told, they can maintain a comfortable existence.
- They become easily threatened by any changes leaders attempt to make that will disrupt the workplace and possibly, their own security.

Leaders remain steadfast in their determination to effect the changes they believe will positively enhance and transform their organizations.

- They expect resistance to their ideas, practices and methods, and that it will create frustrations and impediments to enacting operational or procedural changes.

- They understand that though painful, their actions are necessary and will ultimately be rewarded.
- As their ideas become refined to the point where they take root and develop, leaders derive personal satisfaction from seeing their visions and goals attained.
- Leaders accept the burdens, frustrations and often lack of acceptance that comes with adhering to their beliefs.
- They are continually "tempered in the furnace" of adversity.
- It is this process of refinement that hones their leadership skills and makes them likely candidates for advancement, as compared to most managers taking safer and more secure roads to asserting their influence in the organization.

POINTS TO PONDER — SOMETHING TO THINK ABOUT

1. What resistance or obstacles have you experienced as a leader? What have you done to overcome them?
2. How have you personally handled the resistance and frustrations you have encountered?

TRAINING ACTIVITY — APPLICATION & ACTION PLAN

1. As you continue to develop as a leader, determine what types of roadblocks and obstacles you may encounter along the way. Identify the individuals who may resist your efforts as well as the specific actions they may take to hinder your success.
2. Once determined, identify steps you can take to overcome obstacles and counter bureaucratic resistance.

3

Resistance to Change

One of the biggest challenges leaders committed to reform and innovation face in their organization is opposition to change.

Resistance can take many direct and indirect forms. Most leaders will address symptoms rather than the root causes of resistance. This drains both time and resources while adding to the difficulty, frustration and anxiety of striving to surmount the barriers to change.

People like to work and live within their comfort zones. Operating within these confines lends a degree of personal security. They have familiar surroundings and know what to expect with little or no surprises. Most will do anything and everything to protect their comfort zones from possible interference or intrusion from outside forces.

This tendency conflicts with the fact that for an individual to grow, he or she must get outside of their comfort zone. People often find this a risk not worth taking; this is the root cause of resistance to any organizational change.

The negative effects of this unwillingness to accept risk are compounded by the volatility in which most corporations operate, where economic and competitive pressures compel them to change or flounder. Consequently over the past decade many companies have experienced waves of layoffs, closings and downsizing. This has left "surviving" employees shell-shocked after repeated involuntary and damaging forays outside of their comfort zones. In many instances, rather than an energized and motivated workforce, companies experience higher degrees of individual resistance to change precisely at the time when they need to be more responsive to the needs of a global marketplace.

IMPLICATIONS — WHAT THIS MEANS TO YOU

If leaders only address the symptoms rather than root causes of resistance, they will be frustrated by their inability to overcome barriers to change.

STRATEGIES, TIPS & TECHNIQUES TO APPLY

Anyone in a leadership role needs to understand that opposition to things new is to be expected. Resistance is a natural tendency in people when first introduced to a new idea. In this light resistance should not necessarily be viewed as a negative. In fact, effective leaders are able to harness the power of resistance to their benefit. They understand that resistance is based on two primary factors: risk and trust.

Risk

Any new idea or concept presented to employees is going to be viewed with skepticism because each employee is going to immediately assess the risk to his or her comfort zone. Unless employees can understand that the personal benefit they will receive from a new idea or concept exceeds the level of risk associated with making a change (and a benefit *far beyond* merely keeping their position) they will continue indirectly or directly undermining any initiative that threatens incursion into their comfort zone.

In sales, the key element of success rests in reducing risk in the customer's mind to the point that the benefits outweigh risks associated with making the change (and expenditure) to buy a product. In reducing and minimizing resistance, leaders must do the same.

This is achieved by first recognizing that resistance is going to surface when a change is announced or implemented. Leaders must anticipate this and develop strategies to counter resistance before it distends into a formidable barrier to progress.

Understanding change is a challenge to the employee's comfort zone, leaders must identify and clearly communicate the "pluses" so they can see the benefits will outweigh risks to their personal security. This often means informing employees of how change fits into the overall scheme of organizational change and the reasons why that transition is occurring, such as competitive, global and/or economic threats. They must understand that left unchallenged, the overall threats to the organization can ultimately have a personal effect on the individual employee through downsizing, layoffs and plant closings.

Understanding the risks associated with inaction can be a great motivator and impetus for internal change at all levels. If employees understand the challenges facing their company—and how they can ultimately impact their lives if not addressed—they will work harder to meet and overcome them.

Trust

Leaders may be able to motivate their employees to change, but if there is mistrust of the motives of the leader and the company, resistance will continue.

Management amplifies employee resistance to change when they issue needless, destructive dictates. By laying off employees at the first sign of financial weakness, companies will find it difficult if not impossible to initiate and sustain participative management of any kind. Using employee layoffs as the initial approach to cost reduction contradicts the concept of participatory management. Unless all other cost-cutting alternatives have been carefully considered/exhausted, team spirit and loyalty are not built by releasing the players. Employees who see this occurring will obviously find it difficult to trust the company and commit to its mission.

Leaders themselves may have contributed to an atmosphere of mistrust by failing to sell their employees on their vision and involve and empower them in the process of change. More importantly they may have violated their personal trust in their words and actions.

Without an atmosphere of trust on all levels of the organization, employees will associate an even greater personal risk with change, entrench themselves in their comfort zones, and actively fight any threat, real or perceived.

These reactions can be emotional and lack basis in any form of logic, but without an established and sustained level of trust, resistance will be difficult to overcome.

POINTS TO PONDER — SOMETHING TO THINK ABOUT

1. Have you personally connected resistance to change with challenging individual employees' personal comfort zones?
2. Have you communicated and sold your employees on how change will benefit them to the point where benefits outweigh any personal risk?

TRAINING ACTIVITY — APPLICATION & ACTION PLAN

1. As you begin to implement new ideas and concepts within your unit or division, become more aware of internal resistance to changes or transformations.
2. Identify the risks that employees perceive as personal threats to their comfort zones and sense of security.
3. Determine whether issues of trust are increasing employee resistance.

4

Losing Control of the Process of Change

The process of organizational change is complex. A number of associated factors have the ability to impact the organization's overall ability to successfully evolve. Improper development, management and monitoring can result in the change process spinning out of control and creating chaos. In the center of this storm, it is the leader who must then wrestle control of events and restore order.

As individuals are making the shift from a management to leadership style, the entire workplace is being buffeted by change. The leader is no longer controlling the employee's actions, but guiding and directing them through involvement and empowerment. Properly executed, this should be a smooth transition. However, ill-conceived plans implemented by poorly prepared leaders and employees can turn the entire process into chaos.

IMPLICATIONS – WHAT THIS MEANS TO YOU

Most organizational changes do not transpire quickly. Typically, organizations and leaders both evolve together as they transition from one style of management to the other. Leaders grow through the persistent application of leadership ideas and concepts and development of their skills. The process is without an ending point, and continually moves forward over time.

STRATEGIES, TIPS & TECHNIQUES TO APPLY

Leaders who find themselves in the midst of a process that has swirled out of control must not be swept away by the tide of events and circumstances. If they are, they will give up the ability to remain detached and view what is happening objectively. This can be challenging because they must regain control while dealing with the daily demands and pressures of the job. Because of this they must understand that they are staring down a complex and often daunting task. For the leader in these circumstances, the first step is to retain or regain emotional control and then proceed dispassionately.

Identify Causes

It is simplistic to think a single cause of a complex problem can be identified. Most problems are caused by ever-widening and overlapping circles of circumstances and events. What appears to be an obvious and clear-cut cause is often only symptomatic of a much deeper problem. When events appear chaotic, the problem can lie in more than one area and each has to be addressed in turn.

Leader's Role

While real introspection is often painful, a leader has to identify any possible personal contributions to the problem. Chaotic events often occur for reasons directly stemming from the leader. In certain instances the leadership role was thrust upon an individual lacking the aptitude and confidence to fulfill it. Once in the position, they fail to lead and are unable to manage due to the organizational change, and consequently leave a vacuum that is filled by disorder.

In other instances, the leader may be new and inexperienced and is attempting to accomplish overly ambitious goals and objectives. Rather than evolve, they are pushing change too fast or expecting too much of their employees.

Employee's Role

When the process seems to be collapsing, the employee's role must also be examined. In certain instances employees did not receive adequate training to fulfill the roles expected of them. In other cases too much is expected of employees too quickly. They are immediately overwhelmed and unable to deal with the circumstances.

A lack of employee involvement and empowerment in the process can cause major setbacks. Their lack of input and feedback did not foster the ownership of ideas and participation. Consequently, they perceived too high a personal risk, which created resistance. Since their involvement is essential, this created a void that was quickly filled with chaos.

The Plan's Role

Consideration must be given to whether the plan underlying the process itself may be flawed. This can happen for a variety of reasons brought about by both the leader and employee's participation (or lack thereof) in its development. Motivation, beliefs, resistance and lack of skills and/or experience can give rise to a poorly conceived plan. Typically, such problems associated with either leadership's or employees' role in the process will impact the overall plan.

Timing and Timetable

Ill-conceived timing and timetables can wreak havoc. Inexperienced leaders might not be aware of the impact of certain change implementation dates on the organization. Additionally, attempts to accomplish too much too fast can overwhelm the entire organization.

The Organization's Role

In certain instances, management can undermine their own efforts by micro-managing the process and issuing counterproductive dictates and mandates. In other circumstances, employees might not trust the motives of the company due to past experiences and existing policies.

Lack of management and financial support of the process undermines employees' ability to accomplish their goals and objectives. Without proper support, leaders' efforts will be severely hampered.

Question the Premises

Leaders must question the rationale and premise for the process of change. Based on their current experience, they must revisit the assumptions, facts, data and other key factors identified at the beginning of the process. They must determine if the logic and thinking behind the process is still valid in light of their experiences.

Determine Solution

Once the causes have been isolated, leaders are often forced to begin the entire change process again. However, now they have identified the sources of the problem and have learned from the experiences of past failures. With this base of knowledge and expertise, they should be able to streamline the process and eliminate many of the bottlenecks. However, if they have not addressed the causes honestly and objectively, many of the same problems will recur.

Implement Plan

Once control has been regained, implementation of the process should proceed more cautiously, assuring that a solid foundation for change is established and that each step is successfully and competently achieved before moving ahead with the next.

Astute leaders should enlist the assistance of key influencers within their employee pool. These are the natural leaders who have the ability to persuade others and enlist their support. If these individuals are sold on the idea of change and understand that the benefits more than offset the risks associated with change, they will be able to convince others within their ranks of the same—and make the leader's job much easier.

The leader should also ensure his or her employees have been properly trained in the necessary skills to do the job. Once they have achieved this level, they should be involved and empowered to participate and control the process from within their organizational unit.

POINTS TO PONDER – SOMETHING TO THINK ABOUT

1. What unanticipated problems or concerns have surfaced during the process of change within your department or unit?
2. Are there any areas that you feel can become a possible liability in effecting the desired change(s)?

TRAINING ACTIVITY – APPLICATION & ACTION PLAN

1. Whether or not you are experiencing problems as your organization proceeds through a change transformation, review the following areas and determine strengths and weaknesses in each.
2. Pinpoint and identify potential problems and needed adjustments.
    - Leader's Role
    - Employee's Role
    - The Plan's Role
    - Timing and Timetable
    - The Organization's Role
    - Question the Premises

5

Reacting Positively to Negative Feedback and Criticism

As facilitators of change within their workplace, leaders must expect negative feedback or criticism from both employees and superiors. Typically, most of this feedback will have its origins in resistance to change, its consequences, or the pace at which it is occurring.

Individuals that have assumed leadership roles must anticipate and handle a degree of criticism.

IMPLICATIONS — WHAT THIS MEANS TO YOU

As leaders begin to direct and facilitate change, they want to be as competent in their leadership role and as successful in desired outcomes as possible.

Positive feedback is always welcome because it reinforces the role and position the leader has taken. However, a problem can arise when negative feedback or criticism surfaces. If the leader perceives he or she is doing an exceptional job, negative feedback or criticism in any form can be deflating. The natural tendency is to become overly defensive. Allowing defensiveness to take hold creates a situation where leaders fall short in being able to test negative feedback for its accuracy and validity.

Defensiveness jeopardizes a leader's role and position in several ways. It openly acknowledges a limitation on his or her personal growth and a definite weakness in their personal leadership principles and beliefs. Defensiveness sends a mixed message of working together to reach the same goals, but only when things are going smoothly and their position or reasoning is not being threatened. More importantly, a defensive posture inhibits modeling leadership wisdom and direction.

Any form of negative feedback or criticism does contain valuable information a leader can use to help hone and polish their skills. True leaders seek it out and recognize their dependence upon it. A defensive posture not only limits leadership growth but also deepens the employee or superior concerns voiced.

STRATEGIES, TIPS & TECHNIQUES TO APPLY

Negative feedback and criticism is going to be received no matter how well a leader performs his or her job. In dealing with people, there will always be someone who disagrees with a leader's actions, intentions or direction. When negative feedback or criticism occurs, specific techniques are required to handle them.

Perform an Attitude Check

The success or failure of handling criticism is directly related to a leader's personal attitude as to how each receives, views and values this feedback. How leaders react to criticism is analogous to viewing themselves in a mirror. It helps them see themselves the way others do, whether good or bad.

Often the immediate reaction is that criticism is a personal attack, which obviously elicits a negative response. This increases the likelihood of blaming situations and circumstances on others. Criticism received at the same time other crises are erupting can also be exponentially more difficult to handle constructively. However, failure to respond objectively in any situation diminishes a leader's strength.

Further, not every individual is skilled at the art of providing constructive feedback. Often the tone and feel of what is communicated is different from the party's intention. Because it may come out negatively, leaders must take a moment to perform an "attitude check" to make sure that they are open-minded about what, how and why something is being said. This can be difficult, but leaders must learn how to accept and respond to criticism in a way that does not undermine their authority.

Separate Facts from Opinion

Criticism often takes the form of opinion delivered in broad statements. Nothing can be accomplished without separating facts from personal views and unearthing specific reasons why it is being offered. Leaders should take time to question these statements and uncover the reasons or facts behind them.

Acceptance of broad statements without localizing specific details that either substantiate or disprove the feedback only leads to miscommunication and possible emotional responses from both parties. This can deepen the problem because it confuses and muddles the issue being addressed.

Focus on Specific Details

Leaders must focus the conversation on objectively addressing concrete facts. Points must be carefully listened to, analyzed and weighed before responses are given.

If the other party refuses to back up his or her criticism with specific supporting facts, then it is safe to classify their objection as opinion. At this point, the leader must evaluate the credibility of the person providing the feedback, determining if his or her statements have a basis in reality or are merely framed by a personal agenda.

Remove Personal Biases

The nature and principles of leadership demand that individual leaders remove personal and emotional bias from the conversation. When views are being expressed, individual personalities should not come into play and be used as a means to judge the accuracy or validity of what is being said. Separating personalities from the information being communicated assures that the leader remains objective and focused on the issues.

In circumstances where strong emotional responses are vented, it is beneficial to allow the other party to air their concerns and frustrations while listening carefully to them. These issues can then be logically addressed and responded to in a more positive way. Doing this builds a better relationship and rapport that works to deepen the individual's respect for the leader.

Determine Validity

Leaders must verify concerns presented as fact to determine if criticism is warranted. Often individuals will twist facts to suit their agenda, basing them on their own interpretations of reality. It is important to openly and objectively analyze all facts so they can be understood and accepted by both parties. Leaders must ask questions to define whether statements are accurate or merely formed from misguided assumptions.

If the feedback is valid and based on a realistic assessment of a situation, it should be used to form the basis of a discussion. Valid facts and truth are the starting point for assessing and determining possible responses to feedback.

Modify if Warranted

Leaders understand there will be elements of truth to any negative feedback. In many cases, comments will highlight areas that could use additional attention. At times leaders may have to face the reality that their own personal actions or behaviors have justified critical feedback. At this point, they need to assess their decisions or actions that may be directly linked to the comments or issues raised.

When leaders close their minds and ears to what is being said and discount any form of criticism, they greatly hinder their chances of success. The key is for leaders to learn from experience and, if required, make necessary modifications or changes related to employees' or superiors' feedback.

POINTS TO PONDER — SOMETHING TO THINK ABOUT

1. How well do you handle constructive negative feedback, especially angry, frustrated criticism made without basis in fact?
2. Are you open to employees' critical feedback or do you tend to dismiss what they have to say? Do you react in the same way when superiors offer criticism?

TRAINING ACTIVITY — APPLICATION & ACTION PLAN

1. Think of several types of criticism or negative feedback you have received in the recent past.
2. Use the following points to filter the feedback and glean positive information from it.
    - Perform an Attitude Check
    - Separate Facts from Opinion
    - Focus on Specific Details
    - Remove Personal Biases
    - Determine Validity
    - Modify if Warranted

6

The Challenge of Handling Conflict

Conflict in the workplace is often created when somebody wants to make a change another party does not agree with. Often it only takes one to create controversy. This person draws others—who many times in order to maintain the relationship have no option—into the vortex. Since this can lead to these people then terminating their employment with the company, the conflict must be resolved.

The role of the leader includes mediating conflicts between employees. Many leaders not confident in their ability to resolve stressful conflict may seek to overlook, minimize, or avoid it altogether, allowing it to fester and grow through backbiting and constant complaining that saps the productivity of the organizational unit.

In some cases, unresolved conflict may mushroom into a legal issue with one or more parties using attorneys to resolve the problem. This often has wide-ranging ramifications for both the company and the involved leader.

IMPLICATIONS – WHAT THIS MEANS TO YOU

It is important for leaders to understand that conflict and disagreements are part of the workplace environment and that it is in everyone's best interest to develop the skills to resolve these disputes quickly and equitably. Effective leaders learn to watch for any potential conflicts and quickly address the pertinent issues before they explode into a bigger problem. Conflicts and disputes are best addressed early on before they become more complex and difficult to handle.

STRATEGIES, TIPS & TECHNIQUES TO APPLY

"Conflict" is used to describe numerous situations that are not in fact conflicts, but problems of indecision and personal stress. Conditions induce workers whose jobs are interdependent to feel angry and perceive others as being at fault. These situations and reactions constitute a business problem that must be resolved.

What Causes Conflict

There are seven types of conflicts. The leader who can develop a clear understanding of the issues greatly reduces the likelihood of mismatching problems and solutions.

Leaders should understand that most conflicts are complex and can include several elements of different issues. Leaders must carefully observe to determine the actual issues involved in order to match causes with solutions.

Data

Data conflicts arise over facts, figures and statistics and will have their solutions in obtaining new data or verifying and clarifying existing data.

Personality

Where there are people there will be personality conflicts. While in general a person cannot hope to please everyone all of the time, the problem is often directly attributable to the manner in which parties interact with one another and can be addressed by improving communication between involved parties. This may include clearly stating needs and developing clear expectations or even written agreements between conflicting parties.

Values

Clashes over values occur when disagreeing parties have real or perceived incompatibilities in their personal belief systems. Solutions include increased tolerance, understanding and acceptance of opposing points of view.

Resources

Disputes often arise from struggles over a real or perceived scarcity of available resources to adequately perform a job or achieve objectives.

'History'

Conflicts can stem from unresolved experiences, problems and issues. These conflicts can only be settled by revisiting the past. Issues were created over time, and as such will take time to resolve. Both parties must be allowed to vent their frustrations and perspectives on the issue. The separate issues identified must be addressed and trust reestablished between the conflicting parties.

External Sources

External conflicts refer to the realities of life outside the workplace including anxiety over childcare, health, finances, divorce and other personal issues.

Psychological

These conflicts are caused or maintained by the psychological needs of individuals including the desire for power, control, autonomy and recognition. Psychological issues are often masked by other more tangible problems and may be difficult to distinguish. These issues can only be resolved by addressing the individual's psychological needs.

Common Responses to Conflict

Individuals in conflict will normally employ one or more of the following three basic responses.

Fighting

When an individual chooses to fight, they are taking a side and getting caught up in the emotional energy flying around the dispute. These individuals are only in touch with their personal feelings and those on their side of the dispute.

A fighting response may be appropriate when a legal point must be decided, the moral issue is at stake or when a clear victor will not damage the relationship between conflicting parties.

Avoidance

Individuals who engage in avoidance are trying to protect themselves from conflict by erecting psychological barriers. This is their way of handling conflict from a safe distance. These individuals have difficulty empathizing with other parties due to the distance they have created between them.

Avoidance may be appropriate when it is important to allow the conflict time and space to de-escalate.

Acquiescence

Individuals simply give up and drop their demands when faced with a conflict. Most feel it is not worth the fight, but may feel used and manipulated later on. The problem is unresolved and festers until it erupts at a future date.

In other cases, individuals acquiesce because they prefer to give up on smaller issues to win when larger problems arise.

Resolving Conflict

The most effective means of settling conflict is to bring all parties together and allow them to air their side of the issue. Leaders must carefully listen to and observe the interaction between conflicting parties and identify the specific mix of issues involved.

Once the true issues are on the table, each must be individually resolved as outlined above. Leaders must be careful to match solutions to the problem. For instance, a historical conflict cannot be resolved by addressing psychological issues nor can a relationship conflict be resolved by addressing value issues. Solutions must take into account the underlying issues of the conflict.

Leaders must take care to completely resolve each issue to both parties' satisfaction. Any issue left unresolved will fester and return as a bigger problem in the future. This includes any conflict with a forced resolution that one or more of the parties is compelled to accept.

POINTS TO PONDER – SOMETHING TO THINK ABOUT

1. What is your personal response to conflict? How does your response affect your ability to resolve conflicts among your employees?
2. How have you typically handled conflict among your employees?

TRAINING ACTIVITY – APPLICATION & ACTION PLAN

1. Select two conflicts you recently mediated among employees.
2. Using the following list, isolate each conflict by specific type and issues.
3. Determine if you resolved each to the conflicting parties' satisfaction.
4. If you found the resolution process did not work, determine what needs to be done in order to find more effective solutions and prevent unresolved issues from resurfacing.
    - Data Conflicts
    - Relationship Conflicts
    - Values Conflicts
    - Resource Conflicts
    - History Conflicts
    - External Conflicts
    - Psychological Conflicts

7

The Leadership Commitment Challenge

Some individuals are thrust into the role of leadership. This can be a challenge in and of itself due to the radical change it brings to their personal and professional lives. Statistics show that 15% of people seek and embrace change, while 70% are reluctant toward it and 15% actively resist it. Therefore within any organization, many individuals thrust into a leadership position are either resistant or reluctant to embrace their new role.

People who acquire rather than seek a leadership role are more likely to be reluctant than totally resistant to the position they are required to assume. While the new role can be overwhelming with its unknowns and issues to contend with, the organization has recognized the individual's talents and abilities, offering him or her performance-based opportunities to learn and develop into a highly effective leader.

IMPLICATIONS – WHAT THIS MEANS TO YOU

Reluctant leaders must understand they have an increased responsibility to their employees as well as their organization to get things done and done well. If they fail to assume and make a personal commitment to their leadership role, resistance to the direction the organization takes is created, causing complex developmental failures.

One single uncommitted or reluctant leader can create an energy drain that is both distracting and debilitating within the organization. If individuals thrust into a leadership role wish not to take advantage of the opportunities presented, they should request an alternate position more within their comfort zone.

When individuals fight against the responsibilities of leadership, their actions, attitudes and behaviors ultimately trickle down, tainting others' contributions and overall desire to become an active part of the organization's success.

STRATEGIES, TIPS & TECHNIQUES TO APPLY

Leadership reluctance is most often caused by fear, uncertainty and doubt. This is the polar opposite of the tough-minded optimism needed to sustain change. Reluctant leaders in changing situations experience internal fear due to a feeling of possible failure and exposed incompetence.

Reluctant leaders often refuse to believe that though the world is tough, they still have the ability to effect real, positive change. Their pessimism and cynicism make the acceptance of the reality and opportunity of change impossible. In an increasingly complex and volatile world they are not realistic and enthusiastic about future possibilities, and hope things will remain unchanged.

The following factors need to be considered by leaders who fall prey to leadership reluctance, but have a serious desire to overcome it.

Attitude

A leader's positive personal attitude, expectations and dedication to their role all work to establish what happens and what gets accomplished within their sphere of influence. These variables have a great deal of influence on the leader's success because they generate feelings of achievement and accomplishment in their employees.

Conversely, their beliefs distorted by pessimism and cynicism, a reluctant leader fails to believe in the possibility of achieving goals, objectives and unit success. They cannot commit to a change they feel will never occur.

As it is therefore their outlook that makes all the difference, the first step a reluctant leader must take is to perform an "attitude check": if their reluctance stems from an inability to believe in the possibility of success, they must question the reasoning behind their attitudes. They must begin to analyze their own motives that inhibit a positive attitude. This includes developing an in-depth understanding of their personal fears and beliefs that—if let stand—will negatively impact their careers.

Commitment

A reluctance to embrace and commit to change is an acceptance of failure. Once this attitude takes hold, leaders fail to adhere to the fundamental principles of success. Amidst the pressures and demands of the position, personal insecurity and anxiety leads to aggression. To the further detriment of employee guidance and direction, any leadership authority that did exist is lost. Resentment sets in as both the leader and his or her employees begin to suffer from an even more pronounced lack of enthusiasm.

Companies cannot legislate commitment: they can require it, but cannot force an individual to make one. Commitment is a state of mind and individual choice. A forced commitment creates resigned, half-hearted efforts—and resentment. Individuals must be given the opportunity to make a choice. When a reluctant leader chooses not to make a commitment, they fall short in believing in themselves, others and the organization. They also fail to take responsibility for their actions.

People have an innate desire to actively contribute and be recognized for their efforts. However, reluctant leaders must understand the gravity and impact of the signals they send. Belief in their abilities will lead to a deeper self-commitment to the challenge at hand. This enhanced personal commitment will then take root and grow in its ability to motivate both them and the people they direct.

Challenges

Leaders are charged with providing their employees an agenda for the future rooted in their organizational and personal vision. This agenda conveys how global changes will affect the organization and present opportunities. Taking advantage of these opportunities requires that all organizational members meet challenges together as a unified force.

Toward this end, leaders show employees how their contributions and designated roles impact the organization. They detail how their concerted, coordinated efforts assist in the achievement of its goals. Numerous surveys support the fact that when employees understand their role and how it affects the success of their organization, they more eagerly and energetically rise up to meet the demands made of them.

Leaders take the same risks as their employees. This includes changing their individual behaviors and giving up a measure of comfort and control that comes with change.

When leaders begin to learn and grow, everything they do tells employees the same opportunities to develop personally and professionally are available to them.

Expectations

Continual change and improvement in an organization requires confident but realistic expectations of what the future holds. Leaders understand no one profits from blind optimism. High hopes and expectations can often be dashed at the first sign of failure. When leaders are reluctant, this failure often begets a feeling of hopelessness and frustration. To rise above leadership reluctance, they must believe in themselves and in their goals. They need to understand that they cannot achieve goals, objectives and their organization's expectations without faith in themselves and the future. The secret is to temper belief in their abilities gained from experience and successes with knowledge that embracing and displaying commitment to change is a difficult but rewarding road to travel.

POINTS TO PONDER – SOMETHING TO THINK ABOUT

1. Does your role as a leader spark your interest, enthusiasm and passion, or do you feel you may be a reluctant leader?
2. Are you personally committed to your leadership role? Is your attitude influenced by your commitment?
3. Are you pessimistic in regard to organizational changes that are occurring or pending? If so, why?

TRAINING ACTIVITY – APPLICATION & ACTION PLAN

1. Make a confidential list of the things you feel cause leadership fears, anxiety and reluctance.
2. Objectively examine each factor and determine which ones are within your power to change.
3. Make a prioritized list of things to work on that will help you develop into a more effective leader.
4. Identify the factors that you feel are beyond your power to change.
5. Detail the level of impact these have on your role as a leader.
6. Eliminate the factors that have little bearing on your personal effectiveness.

8

The Challenge of Overcoming Leadership Failure

It is unrealistic to expect that all leadership endeavors will be successful all of the time. The essence of leadership is that people are going to take risks and fail, learn from those failures, and move on. Yet certain leadership failures that can undermine and paralyze the organization are not at all associated with risk taking, and are entirely avoidable.

When addressing the concept of leadership failure, it is important to discern the reasons and causes behind it. Leadership failure prevents both the leader and their organization from moving forward by creating barriers to taking advantage of opportunities that can increase competitiveness, productivity and market strength. When this happens, the effects trickle down to everyone.

These failures can result from improperly trained leaders, the misapplication of leadership principles, or simply backsliding into old habits.

IMPLICATIONS — WHAT THIS MEANS TO YOU

A leader's knowledge, expertise and leadership skills will be continually challenged in a volatile and complex work environment. Overwhelmed by time constraints and work requirements, leaders can easily create a situation that results in a failure and leadership void.

STRATEGIES, TIPS & TECHNIQUES TO APPLY

Leadership failure is generally the result of succumbing to three essential shortcomings. As they impede their ability to lead consistently, creatively and responsibly, good leaders learn to analyze the factors behind and watch for these hindering deficiencies.

Barriers and unforeseen situations are guaranteed to surface at one time or another. They will test an individual's ability to lead effectively, uncover areas of inefficiency, and succeed. Leaders take preventative actions to ensure they do not succumb to these three leadership faults.

Self-Imposed Barriers

Many leaders find themselves unintentionally creating personal barriers that negatively impact their leadership capabilities and create a void in applying and maintaining their principles and methods. If leaders sense they are falling prey to one or more of the following barriers, they should take immediate action to eliminate them.

- Performing "backseat leadership" or micromanagement including indecisiveness, fence-sitting and avoidance of responsibility.
- Lacking formal, articulated personal and professional goals and a written, detailed plan for how specifically to meet them.
- Lacking positive approaches to serious issues or failing to present suggested solutions to a defined problem.
- Not having a clear understanding of one's own strengths and weaknesses, including not seeking input regarding what they are and suggestions for improvement.
- Believing in a double standard regarding the moral ethics that guide personal and professional lives.
- Not sharing ideas, time, encouragement, respect, compliments and feedback with others.
- Focusing on and criticizing employees' weaknesses rather than building on their strengths and abilities and reinforcing what they do well.

- Not taking one's personal development seriously enough to make a difference.

Not Fully Understanding What Leadership Is and Does

Leaders sometimes forget or have not been properly trained in what leadership is. Its principles and concepts need to be cemented in the leader's thought processes and actions. Not fully understanding the essence, power and influence of leadership as described below often results in failure.

- Leadership is always responsible for everything the organization does or fails to do. It is not a position, title, or manager overseeing his or her employees, but a science and "art" that is constantly applied and refined. It is walking around, motivating, talking and training. It is actively removing barriers to effectiveness through hands-on involvement.
- Leadership understands that the factual basis of the organization continues to change. The thinking that made its success possible yesterday is the same thinking that, if clung to, can result in its failure tomorrow.
- Technology will never replace leadership. The question leadership answers is, "What is an organization going to depend on when technology undermines its competitiveness?" It is dangerous to believe computers and technicians can replace leaders.
- Leadership looks below the surface since both the most promising opportunities and gravest dangers reside there, virtually hidden unless searched out. Leadership also believes frontline employees are a resource, collectively able to identify solid ideas and solutions to an organization's problems.
- Leadership looks beyond the horizon. It acknowledges that success can blind an organization. Leadership skills encourage leaders to be vigilant for changing trends, needs, and possible problems that can hinder an organization's progress.

Assigning Too High a Priority to Goals

Goal setting is a powerful tool—but only a tool. Leaders should not make more of it than it is. Leaders are masters of their goals. Their goals serve them, not vice versa. Leadership failure is often the result of not feeling free to modify their goals at one time or another to reflect what they currently believe is best for themselves or the organization.

Setting specific goals builds commitment to achieving results. However, maintaining an inflexible commitment to a goal is dangerous. The time invested or the costs associated with a specific goal can impair the ability to objectively assess the value of a goal.

Goal setting does reign supreme when it comes to achieving organizational success. However, one way to prevent leadership failure is to never let goals obscure or conceal new opportunities that may prove more valuable. In order to both pursue goals and seek new opportunities, leaders—

- Think strategically every day.
- Realize they are in the business of daily identifying new opportunities and quickly taking advantage of them.
- Encourage their employees to think in terms of, "What if _____?" or, "How could _____?" or, "Why couldn't we _____?" and other possibility expanding questions.
- Talk to others outside the organization to discover their views on future directions.
- Seek information from others different from themselves. Leaders often gravitate toward similar people with similar viewpoints. However, these individuals aren't able to challenge them enough to change the way they think.

POINTS TO PONDER — SOMETHING TO THINK ABOUT

1. What kinds of voids do you see created by leadership failures at your level?
2. Have you ever become overly committed to a goal? What were the results of your inflexibility?

TRAINING ACTIVITY — APPLICATION & ACTION PLAN

1. Identify three new opportunities that you have discovered in your workplace.
    - The opportunities need not be major, only beneficial.
2. Identify the steps that can be undertaken to maximize these opportunities.
3. Determine the impact of realizing the benefits these opportunities hold.
4. Identify and work to remove barriers preventing you from taking action.

About the Author

Timothy F. Bednarz, Ph.D. is CEO of the American Management Development Group, Inc. For over 20 years he has researched, designed and authored hundreds of learning and development programs used by Fortune 1000 companies.

He is also the author of *Great! What Makes Leaders Great. What They Did, How They Did It and What You Can Learn from It* (2011).

Speaking Availability

Timothy F. Bednarz, Ph.D. is available for speaking engagements for your next meeting or association event. He can be contacted at 800-654-4935 or by e-mail at timothy.bednarz@majorium.com.

Bulk Sales

Bulk sales of this book or any other titles available from Majorium Business Press. Inquiries can be directed to sales@majorium.com, or by phone at 800-6654-4935.

Quick Order Form

Fax orders: 715-342-1118. Send this form.

Telephone orders: Call 800-654-4935 toll-free. Have your credit card ready.

Email orders: sales@majorium.com

Postal orders: Majorium Business Press, 2025 Main Street, Stevens Point, WI 54481, USA.

Please send the following books:

____

____

____

____

Please send more FREE information on:

❑Catalog ❑Speaking/Seminars ❑Mailing Lists ❑Consulting

Name: ____________________________________

Address: ____________________________________

City: ____________________ State: _____ Zip: __________

Telephone: __________________________________

Email address: ________________________________

Sales tax: Please add 5.5% for products shipped to Wisconsin addresses.

Shipping by air:

United States: $4.00 for first book and $2.00 for each additional product.

International: $9.00 for first book; $5.00 for each additional product (estimate).

Made in the USA
Monee, IL
21 April 2025

16129837R00033